THE ULTIMATE GUIDE TO CANDLESTICK CHART PATTERNS

STEVE BURNS

ATANAS MATOV

The historical chart patterns in this book were graciously provided by **TrendSpider.com**

DISCLAIMER

This book is meant to be informational and shouldn't be used as trading advice. All traders should gather information from multiple sources, and create their own trading systems. Always consult a registered investment advisor before conducting trades. The authors make no guarantees related to the claims contained herein. Please trade responsibly.

CONTENTS

Foreword   vii
Introduction   ix

1. History of Candlestick Charts   1
2. How to Read Candlestick Charts   4

PART I
Bullish Candlestick Patterns   13

3. Individual Bullish Candles   15
4. Hammer   18
5. Inverted Hammer   23
6. Dragonfly Doji   29
7. Bullish Spinning Top   34
8. Bullish Kicker   40
9. Bullish Engulfing   44
10. Bullish Harami   48
11. Piercing Line   53
12. Tweezer Bottom   57
13. Morning star   62
14. Bullish Abandoned Baby   66
15. Three White Soldiers   71
16. Three-Line Strike   76

17. Three Outside Up   80
18. Three Inside Up   85

PART II
Bearish Candlestick Patterns   91

19. Individual Bearish Candles   93
20. Hanging Man   96
21. Shooting Star   102
22. Gravestone Doji   107
23. Bearish Spinning Top   112
24. Bearish Kicker   117
25. Bearish Engulfing   122
26. Bearish Harami   126
27. Dark Cloud Cover   131
28. Tweezer Top   136
29. Bearish Abandoned Baby   141
30. Three Black Crows   146
31. Evening Doji Star   151

PART III
Neutral Candlestick Patterns   157

32. Neutral Doji Candles   159
33. Marubozu   165

Conclusion   171
Acknowledgments   177
New Trader U   179

FOREWORD

When I first entered the stock market at age 12, it was because my dad wanted me to "buy a few things to hold on to", to see what would happen. I quickly blew that account and a few more after that. When I started as a market participant, I didn't know what a price chart was, and I definitely didn't know what a candlestick was (other than what was sitting on my parent's dining room table). I didn't start looking at candlesticks until my college years, and I quickly realized that I had been trading without important price information. I now use hollow candles on every chart to see the constant battle between buyers and sellers in each time frame.

Fast forward 16 years later, and it's hard to believe that I can call one of the best in the business a friend and business partner. From my first conversation with Steve, I knew he was a genuine person that was focused solely on finding the best platforms out there to help new and seasoned traders. I was honored he would take the time to check out TrendSpider. As time passed, we became close with Steve and were fortunate to receive his feedback on our product to make it better for everyone.

We are extremely excited to provide the charts for this book and show his readers how they can use TrendSpider to learn the patterns discussed here. As you enter the world of candlestick patterns, know that a lot of this will be foreign at first, but with the right study habits and the right technical analysis platform, you will find success!

Jake Wujastyk
January 2021

INTRODUCTION

Traders love charts. One of the first steps as a new trader is to choose the type of chart that you will use in your trading journey.

There are many different types of charts to choose from. There are line charts, bar charts, point and figure charts and Japanese candlestick charts, to name a few. As a new trader, you must pick the one that you will use on your own charting platform.

Most charting platforms have a large selection of chart formats to choose from. This lets you pull up a chart and change the format to see what different formats look like on the same chart.

I settled on the Japanese candlestick chart for my trading journey. They are called candlestick charts because they look like candles and display price action periods in the shape of a candle. The price range of a trading period appears as the candle body and consists of the open and the closing prices that mark the highs and lows. Price action that takes place above the highs or below lows of the open and close create the wicks. The wicks that form above and below the opening and closing prices can also be called *shadows*.

A candle by itself tells the story of the opening, closing and intraday price action with a quick glance. To me, they are more visually appealing than other types of charts and do a better job representing price action.

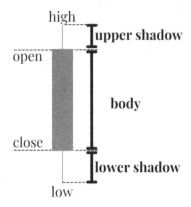

Candlesticks clearly show the opening, closing and trading range of price on a chart and it's easy to see what happened during any trading range. The color designates whether a candle closed lower or higher versus the open, and when using hollow candles, the period close is also compared to the prior day's closing price.

They are colored (depending on the chart format on your platform) showing bullish candles as white or green, bearish candles as red and reversal candles as black. In my experience, the shapes and sizes of the candles and the colors combine to tell a visual story of price on a chart. Bearish price swings lower are indicated in red, while higher, bullish swings are green or white. The larger the candle, the higher the volatility of price action, and the smaller a candle is, the tighter a trading range has become. Increasing candle size indicates expanding volatility, while candles getting smaller shows contracting volatility.

Large wicks that form *above* a trading range show a rejection of higher prices inside the trading period. Large wicks that form *below* a trading range show a rejection of lower prices inside the trading period. Candles capture a trading range inside a specific time period, along with outlying moves, to show how price action played out from start to finish.

The principles of candlestick pattern price action apply to all time frames. Traders use them on their own trading time frame whether it's one-minute, five-minute, ten-minute, hourly, daily, weekly or monthly. Regardless of the time frame, the principles of the patterns they create are the same.

By the time you finish this book, I think you'll agree that for most traders, candlesticks are the best type of charts to use for trading price action patterns.

HISTORY OF CANDLESTICK CHARTS

The precise history of candlestick charting is not clear and there's a lot of myth and legend surrounding their origin. It's commonly accepted that Munehisa Honma (1724-1803) is the father of the candlestick chart. He's believed to have been a rice merchant in 18th century Japan who traded the Dojima Rice market in Osaka.[1]

In 1710, a Japanese rice spot market was transformed into a futures market for rice. The market used coupons for the future rice deliveries. A secondary trading market for coupons emerged in which Munehisa Honma created the first candlestick charts from the historical price action. Stories from the time say that he created a personal communication network of men that were spaced approximately 6 kilometers apart for more than 600 kilometers, between Sakata and Osaka. He used this communication network to track market prices as close to real-time as possible. Theoretically, one of the world's first day traders.

He is believed to have written and published one of the first trading books in 1755, The Fountain of Gold, The Three Monkey Record of Money. It's considered to be the first trading book to address market psychology and trading psychology. In the book, Munehisa Honma explains that understanding the psychology of the market is critical if a trader is to be successful, and that emotions control prices. By identifying market sentiment, a trader can take a position against an extreme move in one direction. According to him, when all are bearish, there's cause for prices to rise, and vice versa. He was the first known advocate of buying the dip and selling the rip.

He explained the rotation of capital through a Yang bull market and Yin bear market, and taught that within each type of trending market, there's a smaller formation of the opposite type. In addition to price action filters, he was reported to have used weather and the volume of the rice market trades.

According to Steve Nison who brought candlestick charts to the West, classic candlestick charting was first developed in Japan after 1850. Although Munehisa Honma is credited with the invention of the first candlestick chart, it's likely that his original ideas were changed, modified, adapted and refined over the past two centuries to give us the candlesticks charts we use today.

While It's difficult to separate myth from history, candlesticks have a great backstory that adds to their mystique.

---

1. https://en.wikipedia.org/wiki/Candlestick_pattern#History

2

HOW TO READ CANDLESTICK CHARTS

A candlestick is a type of chart used in trading as a visual representation of past and current price action in specified time frames.

Depending on the time frame of the chart, each candlestick consists of minutes, a day, a week or a month trading range. On an intraday chart, a candle might represent periods of time like 1-minute, 5-minutes, 15-minutes or one hour. A daily chart shows candles that represent each day's trading range. A weekly chart shows candles that represent each week's trading range. A monthly chart shows candles that represent each month's trading range.

Note that during the day, a daily candle will change as the range changes and price reaches a final, closing position. Similarly, during the week and in the middle of the month, the candles in those time frames are still changing and are not finalized until their time frame closes. At the end of the day, week or month, the candle for that time period is finalized.

A candlestick consists of the *body* with an upper or lower *wick* or *shadow*.

Most candlestick charts show a higher close than the open as either a green or white candle. The opening price as the bottom of the candle and the closing price as the high of the candle body. Also, most candlestick charts show a lower close than the open represented as a red or black candle, with the opening price as the top of the candle body and the closing price as the low of the candle body.

Price action that happens outside the opening and closing prices of the period are represented by the wicks or shadows above the body of each candle. Upper wicks represent price action that occur above the open, while the closing prices and the lower wicks represent price action that occurred below the opening and closing prices.

Candlesticks are one type of chart that can be used in technical analysis to look for repeating patterns and should be used in correlation with other technical indicators and signals. They are combined in many patterns to study the behavior of traders and investors to create good risk/reward trading setups.

Candlestick charts have different settings. Candlesticks can be set to be green/red or they can be set as hollow candles. With the green/red settings, the green candles occur when price closes higher than the previous close and red candles occur if price closes lower than the previous close.

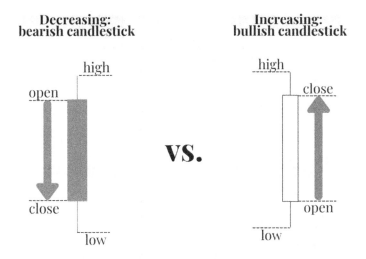

Hollow candlesticks are made up of four components in two groups. First, a close lower than the prior close gets a red candlestick, and a higher close than the previous close gets a white candlestick. A candlestick is hollow when the close is above the open and filled when the close is below the open. This image illustrates the four possible hollow and filled candle combinations when using hollow candlestick chart settings.

coloured candlestick combinations

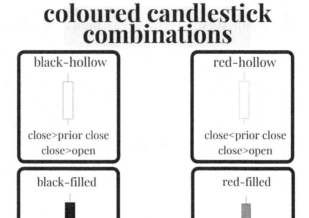

Red, hollow candlesticks can show some bullish reversal price action on an overall bearish chart. Even as the closing price was lower than the previous close making the candle red, the price action moved higher during the period after the open, making it hollow. Even though it closed lower than the previous trading period, there was buying pressure near the lows that made it close higher than the open.

The solid black or grey candle is the inverse price action of the red, hollow candle. Even though the closing price was above the previous close making it black, price action did finish lower than the open to make it a black-filled candle. Even though a black-filled candle closes higher on the current period versus the previous period, it does show selling pressure after the opening price. This candle shows rejection of intraday highs and can be a standalone signal of a bearish reversal during an upswing or uptrend in price action, especially near new highs in price.

There are four types of hollow candlesticks:

- Hollow candles occur when the price closed higher than it opened.
- Filled candles occur when the price closed lower than it opened.
- White candles occur when the price closed higher than the prior close.
- Red candles occur when the price closed lower than the prior close.

Note that white candles have black or grey outlines that may also be called hollow black candles or hollow grey candles.

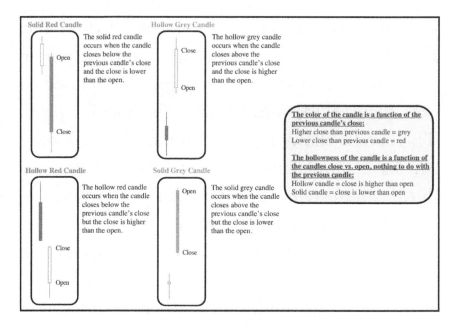

Image courtesy of Jake Wujastyk of
TrendSpider.com

Learning to read candlesticks is like learning a new, technical trading language. With time and experience, a trader can use candlesticks to quickly see current price action. Traders can see the patterns that emerge from buyers and sellers shifting the price action around key technical price levels of resistance and support. In this book, we'll cover bullish, bearish and neutral candlestick chart patterns.

Bullish candlestick patterns have better odds of success when they occur on a chart and have confluence with other bullish signals, like oversold readings, a breakout above a key price support or resistance area, or retaking an important moving average.

Bearish candlestick patterns will have better odds of success when they occur on a chart and have confluence with other bearish signals, like overbought readings, a loss of key price support or an important moving average.

Candlestick chart patterns illustrate the present and not the future. They can increase the odds of a trader capturing the next direction of price movement by aligning them in the path of least resistance. Profitable trading is possible if a trader follows the current trend on a chart while letting winning trades run and cutting losing trades short. Additionally, every successful trader will need to implement proper position sizing and practice self-discipline.

I

BULLISH CANDLESTICK PATTERNS

3

INDIVIDUAL BULLISH CANDLES

**candle basics–
bullish candles**

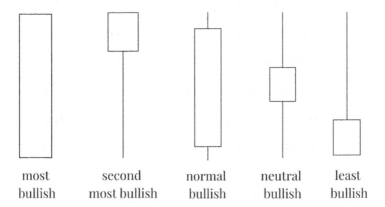

| most bullish | second most bullish | normal bullish | neutral bullish | least bullish |

Individual bullish candles on a chart illustrate buying pressure that drives prices higher from the open to the close. A bullish candle shows that buyers can hold higher prices until the close. The difference in these bullish candles is the movement of price action that takes place between the open and the close.

These patterns can show the possibility of a price reversal during a downtrend, or the continuation of an uptrend already in place. There may be a single bullish candle, or bullish candlestick patterns containing multiple candles in a row.

- The most bullish candle is one that finishes much higher than it begins, near the highest price of the period.
- The second most bullish candle is one that goes much lower in price than it opened, but reverses to finish higher than the open and near the highs of the period by the close.
- A normal bullish candle finishes higher than its open, moves a little

lower than the open and finishes higher by the close.

- A neutral bullish candle closes a little higher than the open after price trades in a wide range throughout the period, going both lower and higher than the open.
- The least bullish individual candle is one that closes a little higher than the open after going much higher in the period, only to close back near where it started.

These bullish candles must be studied contextually based on their chart position in relation to other key technical levels like price support and resistance, moving averages and overbought/oversold readings. A bullish candle has greater significance based on its location inside a larger candlestick pattern.

4

HAMMER

BULLISH

hammer

The hammer is the name used for a single candle pattern that can be a bullish reversal signal when it acts as a reversal signal during a downtrend. Its name comes from the fact that it resembles a hammer, because the short body of the candle is on top of a long wick.

- Many traders believe that to be valid, the lower wick that creates the handle must be at least twice the size of the upper body.
- The body must have a flat top or very little upper range above the closing price, but preferably has no upper wick.
- Hammers have a higher probability of being a valid reversal signal when found inside a chart trending downward.
- The lower wick shows an intraday sell-off, then reversal to close near the highs of the day.
- The hammer candle shows a rejection

of sellers at lower prices inside the period, and demonstrates how buyers eventually take control of the price during the day, moving it higher.

- With the opening and closing prices being near each other, it may show that the intraday volatility to the downside was rejected, and there's a chance for the end of lower lows in the current downtrend.
- After a single hammer candle forms during a downtrend, the next day's candle should open inside the hammer price range, or higher, to confirm that a potential reversal higher did take place.
- Waiting for one more candle to open or close higher after the hammer formation increases the odds that an entry will be successful.
- A longer lower wick can help confirm the price bounce is valid due to the magnitude of the reversal off the lows. Increased volume can also help validate a hammer reversal signal.

- Hammer candlesticks are best used in correlation with other technical signals, like a key previous price support area, a technical oversold bounce or a moving average support for a confluence of buy indicators.
- It has the best chance of success if it appears after a sequence of candles that previously made lower highs and lower lows, and after the hammer appears, the next candles begin to make new higher highs and higher lows.

A bullish hammer can be used as a reversal long signal with a stop loss placed on loss of the low of the day of the hammer candle. If a swing higher in price occurs, a trailing stop can be used to maximize the gain, or a profit target set at a previous price resistance level or an overbought reading.

This Amazon 65-minute chart shows examples of two hammer candles that signal bullish moves. The first occurs inside a range before a swing higher in price. The second hammer has a longer wick handle, and the lows of the hammer hold in the next eight periods before finally moving higher.

Chart courtesy of TrendSpider.com

5

INVERTED HAMMER

BULLISH

inverted hammer

An inverted hammer candlestick pattern is an inverse signal with a long wick on top and the body closing at a higher price than the open. The inverted hammer looks like an upside-down hammer candle.

- An inverted hammer can show the probability of a bottom being in if made during a downtrend, showing a rejection of lower prices when it has a close higher than the lows of the day.
- The inverted hammer pattern is a type of candlestick located at the end of a downtrend, and is used by technical analysts as a bullish reversal signal from the lows.
- The inverted hammer is a one-day bullish reversal pattern because it fails to make lows by the close and shows that volatility has stopped with the small candle body.
- During a downtrend, an inverted hammer price opens lower than the

previous period's low. Price then trades higher, creating a large candle wick inside the period being tracked. It falls from the highs but still closes above the open and finishes trading looking like a square, upside-down hammer.

- The inverted hammer pattern is quantified as a candle with a small lower body along with a long upper wick that's a minimum of two times the size of the small, lower body.

- The candle body must be at the lower end of the price trading range, and there should be a small or no lower wick on the bottom of the candle. There should be little or no price movement below the opening price to create a lower wick.

- A similar pattern to the inverted hammer, although it's the inverse, is formed during an uptrend in price and is called a shooting star. The pattern forms in an uptrend and signals a high probability of a market top. A shooting star generally has a lower closing price than the open and is a bearish signal.

- With the inverted candle, the context of its appearance is critical because it can signal bearishness in an uptrend and bullishness in a downtrend. Even though they look the same, the pattern commonly thought of as the inverted hammer is the bullish version that appears during downtrends, while the bearish version is usually referred to as the shooting star.
- The large upper wick (shadow) of the candle shows that the buyers pushed prices up during the trading period of the candle's formation, but were met with selling at higher price levels. This pushed the price lower, closer to the open than the period highs.
- Many traders wait and look for a higher open and close on the next candle of the time frame to verify the

validity of the bullish inverted
hammer candle, and to increase the
odds of success in buying the reversal
from the lows.
- When using the inverted hammer as a
reversal buy signal, waiting for the
next candle to confirm a move higher
can increase the odds of success.

One potential trade using the inverted
hammer is to buy it at the end of the period as it
forms, and set a stop loss at a price close below the
low of the candle. A trailing stop or price target
can be used to lock in a profitable trade based on
the key technical levels of the chart. To remain in
this long trade, you need to see the price stay in a
trading range with support at the inverted candle
low, or make higher highs and higher lows if it
moves upward.

On this Cisco 65-minute chart, the first inverted hammer candle is followed by an immediate move higher in price before price plunged
the next day. It's important to exit and lock in out-
sized gains when they occur because the risk/re-

ward shifts against long positions after sudden, large rallies to the upside after a move higher has occurred previously. The second inverted hammer candle led to two days of higher prices before the lows were taken out.

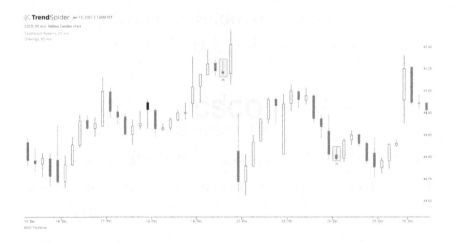

Chart courtesy of TrendSpider.com

6

DRAGONFLY DOJI

A dragonfly doji is a single candlestick pattern where the wick of the candle is much longer than the body. The large wick represents a large trading range during the candle period, and the tiny body represents the opening and closing price being close together.

- This pattern is created when the candle's open, close and high price of a trading period are close together or the exact same. While the intraday trading moved much lower from the open, it reversed back to close near where it started, which is also close to the high of the day.
- A dragonfly doji can act as a signal for a potential reversal in a downtrend of price action if it happens near the lows in price action on a chart.
- The long, lower wick shows that there was selling pressure during the period of the candle. Price reversed strongly to close near the open, as the buyers stepped in at lower prices and

bid the chart back up to where it began.

- This pattern is a signal of a key reversal on a chart during a downtrend, showing that the next swing could be up in price, as lower prices were absorbed and rejected.
- This candle can signal that the lows are in for the chart, at least in the short-term. This candle signals a high probability that the next move will be higher in price.
- A dragonfly doji is a key trend reversal signal and indicator of a change in momentum from lower to higher.
- High trading volume in correlation with the candle increases the probability of success with long positions.
- If a chart has been in a downtrend and moves to a new low in price that's lower than the last three trading days, and fails to hold that low and rallies to close in the upper 10% of the day's overall trading range, it can be a signal

that the chart has begun a new
upswing in price.

One potential entry for a long trade using the
dragonfly doji is to buy on the close as the candle
forms. A stop loss can be set for a close below the
low of the dragonfly doji candle, because that
would invalidate the bullish signal. Winning
trades should be held if the next candles start
making higher highs and higher lows, and a
trailing stop can be used.

Setting a profit target on entry at a key overhead price resistance level on a chart, or an overbought reading, can show a trader if the
risk/reward ratio is worth the trade. Many dragonfly doji candles can present great risk/reward
ratios as they can occur at oversold levels and
signal the beginning of a new swing higher off the
chart lows.

The first dragonfly candle on this Apple 65-
minute chart happened near the top of the price
range, and two days later led to a brief move
higher. The second dragonfly candle happened
closer to the support levels inside the chart's price
period of multiple days, and was followed by a

trading range with no loss of the candle lows before soaring to the upside. Notice that the best
risk/reward ratios for long candle entry signals
occur near a confluence with previous chart support areas, and that the bulk of the gains occurred
on the first, large candle higher.

Chart courtesy of TrendSpider.com

7

BULLISH SPINNING TOP

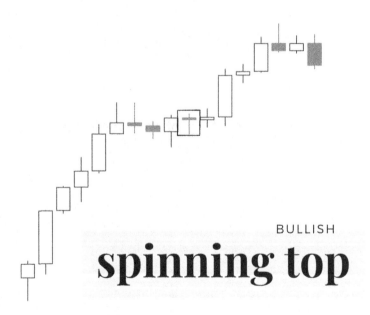

BULLISH

spinning top

A bullish spinning top is a single candlestick pattern that has a body in the middle of two longer wicks. This is a signal that buyers and sellers didn't have total control of price action in the time frame of the candle.

- The spinning top candle indicates that price stopped closer to the open or the close at the end of the time frame than to the extremes of the trading range. This demonstrates that price action is indecisive, and how price closes in relation to the open, and where it happens, can give clues to the upcoming direction.
- The range of the candle's long wick shows volatility and how, at different points in the time frame of the candle, both buyers and sellers had control but failed to follow through and create a swing or trend in price.
- A spinning top candle is primarily used in technical analysis as a signal that a trend is ending. If the spinning

top candle forms after a downtrend in a market's price action, it can signal a good probability of a reversal higher.

- It's an indecision candle with expanded volatility indicating that the current direction of the move on the chart is losing momentum.
- When a spinning top occurs during a downtrend or downswing in price action, it may indicate that sellers are losing momentum and the chart is near a short-term bottom. Inside this context, it's considered a bullish spinning top and is a reversal signal.
- Spinning top candles tend to be nearly symmetrical, with upper and lower wicks of approximately the same size.
- The body of the candle must be smaller than the wicks.
- The pattern shows indecision and greater odds of a reversal of the current trend, or at least the beginning of sideways price action.
- This candle shows buyers losing

conviction in an up move or the charts running out of sellers at lower prices in a down move.

- Many traders wait for one more candle after the spinning top to confirm the reversal and increase the odds that the signal is valid.
- The body of the spinning top candle can be white or black with little difference in meaning. However, bullish spinning tops tend to finish higher than the open.
- Technical analysis can show a higher probability that one thing will happen over another, but there's no substitute for proper position sizing and stop losses to manage risk.
- A move higher in price confirms a bullish spinning top.

A long position can be entered at the end of the bullish spinning top candle with a stop loss set at a close below the candle low. Alternately, a trader can wait for the next candle to confirm the move higher for a greater probability of success.

This delayed entry can trade some of the reward for less risk. After the entry, the next candles should start making higher highs and higher lows in each new period. A chart staying in a price range after a spinning top may indicate that the signal is going to fail. The spinning top can be a reversal signal or show expanding volatility.

In this 65-minute CrowdStrike Holdings chart, the first bullish spinning top candle that happened inside a trading range was followed by a swing higher in price over the next five periods. By contrast, the next two bullish spinning top candles in a row occurred after a large bearish candle, but they were also immediately followed by three large bullish candles higher. In this chart, the bullish spinning top candles were just a pause in the price range before the chart continued moving higher.

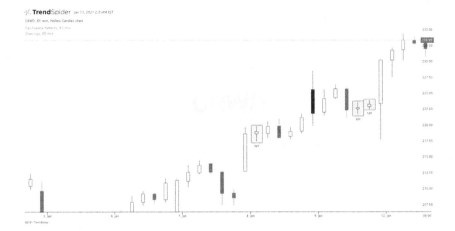

Chart courtesy of TrendSpider.com

8

BULLISH KICKER

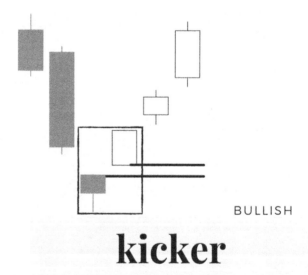

BULLISH

kicker

The bullish kicker candlestick pattern is a two-candle pattern that starts with a large bearish candlestick lower followed by a second large bullish candle that gaps higher in price.

- The bullish candle closes near the highs of the day.
- The bullish candle should have a flat bottom or tiny wick with almost no movement back into the price gap.
- The bullish kicker doesn't have to form after a large downtrend in price, but occurring as a reversal signal can create a better risk/reward ratio.
- This pattern is called a kicker because the price action resembles a football kicker dropping a ball and then kicking it higher into the air with momentum.
- This candle formation shows a change in sentiment from bearish to bullish with no sellers in the gap in price action.
- This candle is similar to the gap and

go pattern in technical analysis and, it's one of the most bullish candlestick chart patterns.

- This pattern is usually created be a news event that suddenly causes the next candle to price the new information into the chart and change the direction of the move.
- The bullish kicker can happen during a price range after a bearish candle or near the end of a downtrend in price. The bullish kicker can be a breakout signal when it happens during a price range and the bullish candle gaps into new all-time highs.
- The bullish kicker is a momentum signal and can also signal a reversal in a downward trend in price.

The bullish kicker is a long signal with better odds of success when it occurs after an oversold reading on a chart. It has less odds of success if it happens after an uptrend in price or the bullish candle moves into overbought territory. If price moves under the low of the bullish candle and back into the gap, the momentum is invalidated and it would signal a need to exit a long position that the pattern signaled.

On this QQQ 65-minute chart, the bullish kicker candlestick pattern was followed by a move higher in price over the next six trading periods before the chart settled back into a higher range.

Chart courtesy of TrendSpider.com

9

BULLISH ENGULFING

BULLISH

engulfing

A bullish engulfing pattern is created when a small bearish black or red body candle appears on a chart followed by a large bullish white or green candle. The larger body that has both a higher high and a lower low is indicated.

- This pattern shows that the lows of the first period were lost in the second period without breaking to the downside, but instead reversed higher.
- This candle shows both a rejection of lower lows, and that there were buyers above the previous day's high that were willing to bid up and hold prices higher into the close.
- The bullish engulfing pattern demonstrates a change of sentiment from an initial bearish move lower at the beginning of the candle's time period to strong bullish buying into that weakness. That allows the price to become strong and close near the high price of the new period. It also breaks above the previous day's high.

- This candle can be a warning to short sellers that they may need to reevaluate their position, because buyers have taken control of the price action and price may not go any lower.
- Although it's most commonly used on the daily chart, it can have meaning in multiple time frames.
- This is a bullish reversal pattern during the end of a downtrend in price.
- When the engulfing candle happens near a short-term support price on a chart, it may show a potential reversal bullish buy signal.

A potential signal to buy occurs as the bullish engulfing candle closes above the previous period high. A stop loss could be set below the lows of the bullish engulfing candle because the pattern would be invalidated. The next candle in the pattern should end up higher than the highs of the bullish engulfing candle.

It's not unusual to see price retrace 50% inside the bullish candle before it goes higher. The important thing to look for is that the lows are not lost, and the chart starts making higher highs and higher lows for the reversal signal to be valid.

This Macy's 65-minute chart shows a perfect bullish engulfing candle pattern after a rally higher. This was followed by a close below the lows of the pattern on the next period candle before trading in a range and exploding to the up-side. A trader may be stopped out prematurely and miss a move, but careful risk management is crucial to keep losses small and survive to trade another day.

Chart courtesy of TrendSpider.com

10

BULLISH HARAMI

BULLISH

harami

A bullish harami is a minimum two candle chart pattern that indicates a downtrend in a chart may be starting to reverse. A bullish harami is commonly formed by a small bullish candle that has a price range inside the previous bearish candle that went lower.

- This pattern can appear to form during a price range, but it has the most meaning when it occurs during a downtrend on a chart.
- It's common for the second bullish candle to be about a quarter of the size of the larger bearish candle that proceeds it. The bullish candle gaps up higher than the previous period's lows, showing a rejection of lower lows before moving a little higher during the period.
- The second candle in the pattern shows bullish sentiment was present as it closed higher than the open. Volatility contracted, and the smaller

trading range shows more agreement by traders at these prices.

- The bullish harami can mark the end of a downtrend because there are no new lows in price that are set. It also signals a high probability that a reversal back to higher prices will occur.

- The word harami comes from a Japanese word meaning to be pregnant. This candle pattern illustrates that a large bearish *mother* candle is *pregnant* with a smaller, bullish *baby* candle.

- When the second bullish candle in this pattern is a doji, it's called a bullish harami cross and indicates that buyers and sellers agreed on the price and were unable to move prices any lower or higher.

- A bullish harami candlestick pattern has better odds of working if it happens on a chart in an oversold area like a 30 RSI, or at a lower 2nd or 3rd

deviation from the 20-day moving average.
- This pattern is a reversal signal in a downtrend that gives a potential dip buy signal.

It may be better to wait for this pattern to show that the next candle will close higher and stay above the lows of the bullish candle to confirm the reversal. A long trade based on this pattern can set the stop loss to a close below the lows of the smaller bullish candle to invalidate the signal. Trailing stops can be used to let a winner run, and profit targets can be projected based on key technical levels on the overall chart to measure the risk/reward ratio of a long trade at entry.

This Microsoft 65-minute chart shows two bullish harami candle patterns that form near the lows on the chart each time. The first is followed by two large price gaps upward, and the second is followed by a range before a slower move higher. This pattern can identify short-term bottoms on a chart. To qualify as a bullish harami in these examples, the candle bodies are inside the previous, larger bearish candle.

Chart courtesy of TrendSpider.com

11

PIERCING LINE

BULLISH

piercing

The piercing line candlestick chart is a two-period price action pattern. It's created after a large downward bearish candlestick is followed by a large upward bullish candlestick. It opens below the low of the preceding candlestick, but closes over halfway up into the previous bearish candlestick body.

- This candlestick pattern is considered a reversal signal when it appears near the bottom of an existing downtrend.
- The piercing pattern happens over two periods when the first candle is created by bearish lower prices, the second candle first takes prices lower than the previous period, but buyers step in to push it back at least 50% up inside the previous day's candle range.
- This reversal shows that the supply from sellers at lower prices has been absorbed in the market by buyers. This sudden demand from buyers at lower prices indicates that there's a

high probability of a bullish reversal, at least in the short-term.

- On a daily chart, the piercing line candlestick pattern typically indicates that price may go higher around a five-day time frame.
- The piercing line is also called the bullish piercing or piercing candle.

A long entry could be made at the end of the bullish candle and held if the next candles kept making new higher highs and higher lows. A stop loss could be placed at a close below the lows of the bullish candle, because that's a low probability area for price to return to after the reversal. A trader entering this trade should be looking for a swing higher in price over the next five days.

On this 65-minute chart, a bullish piercing pattern happens at the lows, followed by a large momentum candle before the chart settles into a higher trading range. Momentum candle signals can lead to large and quick moves, so it's important to have a profit target and/or a trailing stop to lock in profits while they are still there. Fast moves higher can come back down just as fast.

Chart courtesy of TrendSpider.com

12

TWEEZER BOTTOM

BULLISH

**tweezer
bottom**

The tweezer bottom candlestick pattern is created by two or more candles with matching lower lows. A tweezer bottom happens when two candlesticks form back-to-back, or near each other with exactly the same, or close to the same, lows in price.

This pattern is more meaningful when there's a strong move in momentum from the first candle going lower, followed by the second candle going higher off that low, indicating a strong reversal back higher in the price action.

- The two candles that create this pattern don't have to be in consecutive order and the size and colors can be different.
- The tweezer bottom candlestick signal is a high probability reversal signal that is more meaningful when it occurs at a confluence of other signals on a chart, like an oversold reading, price support area or near a key moving average.
- This pattern has additional

confirmation when It's followed by another bullish candle pattern that makes higher highs.

- The tweezer bottom candlestick pattern is a dip buying signal that waits on a high probability bounce as consecutive low prices hold support, with at least two candles confirming buyers are present. A bounce follows, demonstrating that buyers are willing to step in.

- A tweezer bottom can be separated by a few candles, but the classic version of this pattern happens over two consecutive candles.

- A tweezer bottom pattern allows a trader to avoid *catching a falling knife* by waiting for a bounce in price action to confirm that a chart has likely stopped moving down.

- This pattern is like buying a dip, but waits for confirmation that others are also buying the dip. By waiting for a price to hold as support after multiple attempts to go lower before entering, the odds of buying a dip increase.

A long position could be entered on the close of the bullish candle with a stop loss set at the lows of that candle. Support should not be lost if the short-term bottom in price is in.

This pattern is a good setup for a possible buy in near the lows on a chart, at least in the short-term, and can lead to large gains if an upswing or long-term uptrend evolves after the lows.

As with all candlestick pattern entries, It's crucial to cut your loss short if it doesn't work out and to let a winner run with a trailing stop if It's profitable.

This 65-minute Uber chart identifies a tweezer bottom inside a range. It's followed by five doji candles before there's an explosive move into an uptrend in price.

Chart courtesy of TrendSpider.com

13

MORNING STAR

BULLISH

morning
star

The morning star candlestick pattern is created by three candlesticks that show a bullish reversal from the lows in price. Morning star patterns generally form in price action during a downtrend on a chart. It's a signal for a high probability that a low is in and that price is likely to begin to swing higher.

- It's a reversal pattern that indicates that a chart could be going from a downswing to an upswing in price.
- It's a three-candle formation consisting of a bearish down candle first, then a small reversal candle off the lows, and finally a bullish candle that opens higher than the middle low candle, closing closes near its highs of the day.
- The second candle in this formation is usually bullish and has a higher closing price than the open.
- Morning star patterns have more meaning when they happen near previous key price support levels,

important moving averages or oversold technical readings on a chart.

- This candlestick pattern refers to a morning star pattern that has a doji as its middle candle in the three-candle pattern. A morning star can have either a small candle or a doji as its middle candle, because both are valid for this pattern.

- The opposite of the bullish morning star is the bearish evening star, which signals the reversal of an uptrend in price.

- The morning star pattern tries to identify a reversal in downswing in price action by identifying a bounce off the lows, followed by another candle that continues to move higher to confirm that lows held.

- Morning star candle patterns can take many shapes and sizes. As long as the general principles of the pattern are present, they all qualify.

A potential entry signal would be to buy the

third candle in the pattern as it moves higher. A stop loss could be set at the lows of that third candle, because a loss of that level would invalidate the morning star patten bounce signal. This pattern could set up a winning trade to move back to previous price resistance, a key long-term moving average overhead or the 50 RSI depending, on where it occurs on a chart.

This Tesla 65-minute chart shows a morning star candle pattern form at the lows in a price, and is followed quickly by a surge higher in price action over the next eleven candle periods.

Chart courtesy of TrendSpider.com

14

BULLISH ABANDONED BABY

The bullish abandoned baby is a three-candle pattern after a downswing in price. It's created by a large bearish down candle. This is followed by a gap down and a doji, and then a bullish candle after a gap up in price.

- This pattern gets its name from the look of the doji candle getting *abandoned* by the two larger surrounding candles due to the gap down and then back up, which separates the doji from the other two candles.
- This pattern shows that sellers have lost momentum as price stops going down as the doji is formed. Volatility contracts and buyers step in and bid up the price on the next candle.
- This pattern signals a high probability of the end of a downtrend in price and the potential for a move up in price action.
- This pattern can be followed by either a swing back up in price or a new

trading range forming after the reversal off the lows.

- Price should not drop under the low of the last bullish candle in the pattern or it will invalidate the signal.
- The middle candle in the bullish abandoned baby doesn't have to be a perfect doji, but it needs to be a small body candle with long upper and lower wicks that are formed below and outside the range of the preceding bearish and subsequent bullish candle bodies.
- The strong gap down for the middle candle can show an exhaustion gap for sellers as they all exit the trade.
- The small middle candle shows that sellers are no longer exiting their positions and have agreed on the lower price for the period.
- The last candle in the pattern that is bullish shows buyers stepping in to drive the price higher and indicates that selling pressure has been overcome.

- This pattern shows the path of least
  resistance is likely to the upside over
  the next several candles.

The common buy signal for this pattern is at the end of the third candle that is bullish, with a stop loss set below the low of that candle. The pattern is a strong indicator that price is unlikely to go back into the gap formed between the doji and the bullish candle. A long position could be held if the next candles start to make new higher highs in price.

This daily Dineequity chart shows a bullish abandoned baby candlestick pattern before an upswing to new highs in price on the chart. In this chart, the wicks above the doji candle are still considered a gap. This is a powerful bullish pattern and rare to find on a chart, because a pure gap above is not often seen.

Chart courtesy of TrendSpider.com

15

THREE WHITE SOLDIERS

The three white soldiers pattern is one of the most bullish candle signals. It's created when three large bullish candles form in a row, each having higher highs and higher lows than the previous one. This pattern needs all three of these data points across a time frame to signal momentum and an increased probability of a market shift, to an uptrend from range-bound or a downtrend in price action.

- This candlestick pattern looks like a staircase with each open above the previous day's open, and the next candle holding at least the middle price range of the previous period.
- Each candle in this pattern should close at a new higher high than the previous candle.
- The three white soldiers pattern is a strong confirmation for any other momentum signals that the market has shifted to a bullish uptrend.
- This pattern works best with a confluence of other momentum

signals like moving average bullish crossovers, resistance breakouts or the MACD crossover.

- The chances of this pattern not working increase if the strong move higher takes a chart into an overbought reading like a 70 RSI, or over three standard deviations from the 20-day moving average. The odds of it working increases if the move happens off oversold support near the 30 RSI.
- This momentum signal is primarily used as a reversal signal out of a downtrend or a bear market, because that creates the best risk/reward ratio at entry at lower prices that have begun to move higher.
- It can also be a breakout signal from a range when prices move out of a long-term range to new highs in price. The longer the price range, the greater the odds that the new trend will continue to go higher.
- This pattern is for momentum traders

looking for fast price moves to the upside. It should be used in popular growth stocks or charts having strong moves based on high expectations of gains.

- Traders entering on the third bullish candlestick in the pattern should see a fast move continue higher if the trade is going to be successful.

- Trades using this pattern are usually fast momentum trades over a short period of time. A day trader on an intraday chart may only trade this pattern for an hour or less.

- The opposite of this bullish pattern is the three black crows, bearish reversal. In contrast, the three black crows have three strong, bearish candles to the downside, with lower lows and lower highs.

A stop loss should be set to exit if price retraces more than halfway back inside the third bullish candle in the pattern. It's usually best to exit this trade with a profit target to the nearest price resistance or overbought area on a chart while profits are still available. Charts with this much momentum tend to go back down as fast as they go up.

This 65-minute Apple chart shows the three white soldiers pattern at the beginning of what turned out to be a slow trend higher over the next seven trading days. It never went back below the lows of the initial pattern. This can be both a short-term momentum signal or a long-term trend signal, depending on where it occurs on a chart.

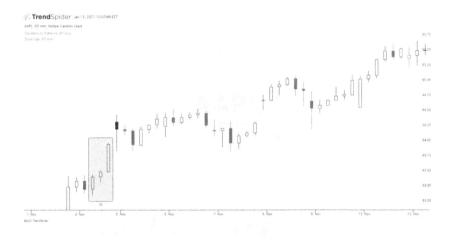

Chart courtesy of TrendSpider.com

16

THREE-LINE STRIKE

BULLISH

three line strike

The three-line strike candlestick pattern is a bullish, dip buy signal that occurs when a large bearish candle follows three smaller bullish candles during an uptrend in price.

- It's a four-candle pattern with each of the three bullish candles having a higher high and higher low, closing near the price range high, with small wicks in each period.
- The fourth candle starts higher than the previous bullish candle and then reverses.
- It has a large bearish move back below the three previous bullish candles, engulfing all of them inside the bearish candle range.
- It then closes lower than the first bullish candle in the pattern.
- The fourth candle makes both the low and the high of the four-candle pattern period.
- The three-line strike candlestick pattern is a powerful bullish signal

because it provides a good dip buying opportunity. This is due to selling as prices return to the lows of three periods ago during an uptrend.

- This pattern signals that there's a possible dip buying opportunity on a chart in the current time frame.
- For dip buyers waiting for lower prices to enter an uptrend, this gives a good support level to enter as the fourth candle closes at a four-day low in price.

A common buy signal for this pattern is at the close of the fourth bearish candle, with a stop loss set with a close below the lows of the candle in the four-period candle pattern.

The lows of the final bearish candle is a good place to set a stop loss and use to exit for a small loss if price continues lower.

This pattern can signal that a low in price is in on the chart, and a long trade can often be held for a longer period as it goes sideways and eventually trends higher. A trailing stop can be used to let a winner run if it begins to trend higher.

In this 65-minute Nvidia chart, after the bullish three line strike pattern occurred, price found support near the lows of the large bearish candle and went sideways for five periods before surging to the upside. Notice that price never closed the period below the lows of the large bearish candle and the surge to the upside was brief.

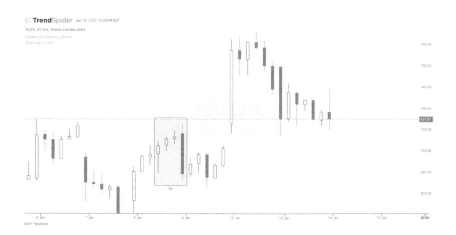

Chart courtesy of TrendSpider.com

17

THREE OUTSIDE UP

BULLISH

three outside up

The bullish three outside up candlestick pattern is a three-candle reversal signal that can appear on charts during downtrends in price. It's formed by a bearish candlestick followed by two bullish candles.

- The first bullish candle is engulfing the previous bearish candle, going both lower than and higher than the first bearish candle range.
- It's followed by a smaller bullish candle that makes a higher high and a higher low, and closes higher than either of the first two candles.
- The three outside up pattern is created by one bearish candlestick, followed by two bullish candlesticks in sequential order with no interruptions, with the first candle down, second candle up, and last candle at the highest point.
- This pattern shows a quick shift in market sentiment from bearish selling to bullish buying and shows a possible

bounce during a downtrend back to
an upswing in price.

- If the bullish candle buying starts in
  confluence to a key price support level
  or important moving average on the
  chart, it increases the odds of this
  reversal being a profitable buy signal.
- The overall chart is in a downtrend of
  price action with lower highs and
  lower lows.
- The first candle to start the pattern is
  bearish.
- The second candle is bullish with a
  long body and completely engulfs the
  first candle.
- The third candle is bullish with a
  higher high and higher low that also
  closes higher than the second bullish
  candle in the pattern.
- It can be a good practice to cover short
  positions if you are short and see this
  pattern form on the chart.

This pattern gives a buy signal on the second
straight bullish candle that confirms the pattern. A

potential stop loss could be set on the loss of the support of the second bullish candle under the lowest price.

This pattern is more for a swing back to previous support that may be the new resistance rather than a new, long-term trend. The 50 RSI on the chart is a good price target if this pattern occurred on an oversold reading like the 30 RSI. This is a reversal signal showing sudden momentum to the upside.

This daily Avista chart shows two distinct, three outside up candlestick patterns. The first occurred before a brief move higher and then failed. The second pattern lead to an immediate and brief move higher with momentum over two periods. It also failed and reversed back to the lows of the pattern. This demonstrates that you must manage trades after entry with stop losses to keep losing trades small and use trailing stops to lock in profits if a reversal begins.

Chart courtesy of TrendSpider.com

18

THREE INSIDE UP

BULLISH

three inside up

The three inside up candlestick pattern is a bullish reversal signal on a chart. It's formed when a large bearish candle is followed by a smaller bullish candle that has its range inside the previous bearish candle. This is followed by a third bullish candle that closes above the previous two candles.

- This pattern signals the potential of a move higher in price in the short-term, and can lead to a swing back to the upside, a new uptrend or sideways price action.
- This pattern only has context in relation to the area it is found in on a chart. In a downtrend, it can be a reversal signal to the upside, in a price range it can signal the beginning of a new uptrend, and in an uptrend it can signal a continuation of the uptrend in price after a pullback.
- This pattern has a much greater chance of being successful as a bullish signal if it forms near price support on

a chart, an oversold area like the 30 RSI or a key long-term moving average like the 50-day or 200-day.

- This pattern begins with a large down candle that shakes out a lot of sellers at low prices.
- The second candle opens higher than the previous lows and holds the lows of the previous day, demonstrating that there are no sellers at lower prices.
- It closes higher than its own open, confirming a potential reversal off the lows.
- This price action signals to existing short sellers it may be time to buy to cover their positions as the lows hold.
- The last candle finishes the pattern and signals new bullish momentum and that lows in price may be in for the current time frame.

This pattern gives a potential buy signal at the end of the third and last candle as it closes higher than the previous two candles. A potential stop loss can be set for the loss of the third candle lows. A profit target for the trade could be set at the 70 RSI and the trailing stop could be a close below the previous day's low if it starts to trend higher.

This 65-minute Starbucks chart shows a bullish three inside up candle pattern that formed right before the price dropped back below the lows of the pattern before reversing higher. Price didn't close below the lows of the total pattern for a period, but did move back under all the candles in the pattern intra-period. This is an example of an entry that would likely lead to a loss without a very wide stop loss set on a period close under the pattern low. Wider stop losses can lead to a higher winning percentage as well as bigger losses with losing trades; it's a tradeoff.

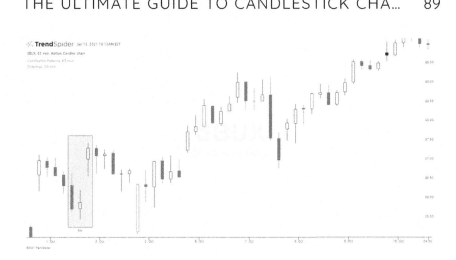

Chart courtesy of TrendSpider.com

II

BEARISH
CANDLESTICK
PATTERNS

19

INDIVIDUAL BEARISH CANDLES

candle basics–
bearish candles

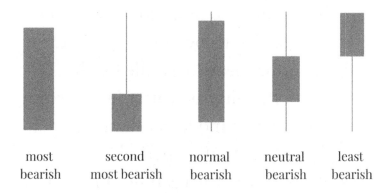

most	second	normal	neutral	least
bearish	most bearish	bearish	bearish	bearish

Bearish candlestick patterns are a visual representation of selling pressure. These patterns illustrate the possibility of a price reversal during an uptrend or the continuation of a downtrend. There are single bearish candles as well as bearish candlestick patterns containing multiple candles in row.

- The most bearish individual candle is one that finishes significantly lower than it began, and closes near the lows of the period.
- The next bearish candle is one that goes higher in price than it opened, but reverses to finish lower than the open near the lows of the period.
- A normal bearish candle finishes lower than its open after briefly being both higher and lower than the open during the trading period.
- A neutral bearish candle closes a little lower than the open, after price trades in a wide range during the period,

being much higher and much lower at some point.

- The least bearish individual candle is one that closes a little lower than the open after going much lower in the period, only to close slightly lower than where it started.

These bearish candles must be studied contextually based on their chart position in relation to other key technical levels, like price support and resistance, moving averages and overbought/oversold readings. These candles can also combine with other bearish and bullish candles to create price action patterns. The bearish candles combine with others to show the best probabilities of the next direction of price. They are visual representations of either a reversal of a current bullish price move or confirmation of continued momentum to the downside.

20

HANGING MAN

BEARISH

hanging man

A hanging man is a type of bearish reversal candlestick pattern. It's a three-candle pattern located inside an uptrend of higher highs and higher lows on a chart. It looks similar to a hammer candle, but it can be identified as based on the context of where it occurs near the top of an uptrend.

- It signals a reversal during an uptrend in price, because the candles before and after it both have lower lows than the candle itself.
- This candle should also have a lower close than open to increase the odds of a reversal materializing.
- The hanging man candle has a lower wick that is typically twice the size of the body.
- The candle top is flat with little or no upper wick. The long lower wick expresses the wide intra-day trading range and volatility. The smaller body shows the open and closing prices were close to each other.

- The lower wick must be at least double the size of the body to be a valid hanging man, and the body must occur at the top of the daily trading range.
- The most valid hanging man candles tend to close lower than their open.
- A hanging man candle appearing during the top of an uptrend increases the odds of a reversal happening and the chart turning to the downside or going sideways.
- Some traders use the hanging man as a standalone signal, but the chances of success increase if it happens at the same time as other technical indicators, like previous price resistance or an overbought reading on the chart.
- It can be visual evidence that buyers are losing the ability to hold price higher and that sentiment is starting to change. It can show that the momentum of an uptrend is starting to wane.

- A hanging man shows the buyers losing the battle to hold prices higher. Even with buyers managing to bid prices back up from the lows by the close, there was selling pressure that dragged prices much lower during the trading period.
- This candle pattern shows the first stage of selling pressure during an uptrend. For traders that focus on candlestick signals, they may want to lock in their long position profits or even sell short after this pattern forms.
- It's often a warning sign for current long positions that a trend is starting to bend and come to an end.
- This candlestick pattern is called a hanging man only when it appears in *uptrends*, it's bearish, and is confirmed by the previous and subsequent candles making a lower low.
- The same visual pattern formed during a *downtrend* is called a hammer candlestick and is bullish in the context of a chart because it shows

a rejection of new lows, and closes
higher than the open.

This pattern can be a short signal on the next candle as it opens lower after the hanging man, or a trader can wait for the close of that candle to sell short. A short position should have a stop loss set on a breach of the high price of the hanging man candle. A profit for the short position should be based on a previous chart price support level or meaningful moving average.

The next candle that confirms lower after the hanging man is frequently a good place to lock in long profits.

This Alibaba daily chart is a perfect example of a hanging man candle pattern. A bullish candle is followed by the hanging man, a bearish candle before a swing in prices to the downside, followed by a gap down five days later and plunge with a pin bar candle that marked the bottom. The hanging man candle was an early warning single before the move to the downside.

Chart courtesy of TrendSpider.com

21

SHOOTING STAR

shooting
star

BEARISH

A shooting star candle or pin bar reversal is a bearish candlestick pattern when it appears during an uptrend on a chart. A shooting star tends to have a long upper wick, almost no lower wicks and a small lower candle body.

- A shooting star usually happens when a stock opens and then goes much higher intra-day, reversing and closing lower, near or below the opening price.
- The larger the upper wick is in relation to the candle body, the more bearish it is. It has created new overhead resistance and shows a rejection by buyers at higher prices.
- A shooting star looks like an inverted hammer but it's bearish in an uptrend. The shooting star candle has a lower close than the open and is commonly a red or black candle.
- A shooting star is a bearish signal and could indicate the end of an uptrend

and the increased possibility of an upcoming downtrend.

- It's bearish because it shows the rejection of higher prices and the beginning of selling pressure.
- If the next candle after the shooting star has a lower high and lower low, it may be signaling the end of the uptrend.
- The candle before and after the shooting star should both be bearish to increase the odds of a reversal during an uptrend to lower prices.
- Shooting star candles are best used in confluence of other signals like overbought readings, key moving averages or resistance zones.

A shooting star can be a good time to look at locking in profits on any long positions during a strong uptrend, especially if it occurs at overbought areas like the 70 RSI or the 3rd deviation from the 20-day moving average.

A short position initiated at the close of the shooting star or the next bearish candle should have s stop loss placed at the highs of the shooting star candle, because price closing back over the high of the period negates the bearish signal. A trailing stop could be moved to each previous candle high as an end of period stop. A price target could be set at an old resistance level or the 50 RSI on the chart.

This shooting star candle on the Raytheon daily chart that appeared inside the trading range gave an early signal of an impending downturn. However, the chart briefly moved higher for two out of the next three days before moving lower.

This is an example of a candle being correct, but moving against the immediate candle entry signal, likely leading to a short seller being stopped out. It would have been a good exit signal for long positions four days before the chart sold-off. Notice that after the shooting star candle, the chart failed to create an uptrend for the next five weeks.

Chart courtesy of TrendSpider.com

GRAVESTONE DOJI

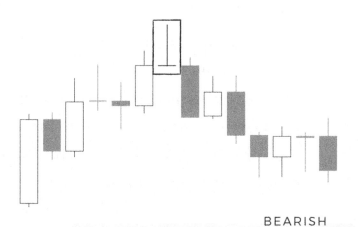

BEARISH

gravestone doji

The gravestone doji candlestick pattern is generally a three-candle pattern. The first candle in the pattern is usually a large bullish candle. It's followed by the second gravestone doji candle that has a long top wick with the closing price near the same price as the open and near the low of the period. The last candle in the pattern is generally a large bearish reversal lower.

- These three candles show a rally, then a failed move higher, and finally a reversal to lower prices.
- The long upper wick on the middle candle shows that sellers came in during the trading period to reject further upward movement to higher highs in the trend. This can be a signal that the uptrend is ending and reversing and going back down or beginning to go sideways as upward momentum has been lost.
- A gravestone doji candlestick pattern can be a signal to take profits on a long

position as it shows the uptrend could be ending.

- It can also be used as a signal to enter a short position, betting that the odds are that prices fall lower.
- This is a bearish reversal signal during a bullish uptrend and should occur near the current highs on a chart.
- Gravestone doji candles that occur inside price ranges have less probabilities of signaling a reversal.
- The odds of the gravestone doji increase when it happens in overbought territory on a chart and near the highs. It shows extreme profit taking and a lack of buyers at higher prices.
- This is one of the strongest bearish reversals that can occur on a bullish chart.
- The opposite of a bearish gravestone doji that occurs near the top of a chart is a bullish dragonfly doji which happens near the lows on a chart.
- The name *gravestone* comes from the

image of this pattern marking the death of a bullish uptrend and the beginning of a new bearish downtrend.

It may be prudent to lock in profits in long positions at the end of the gravestone candle at the end of an uptrend. A new short position could be initiated at the close of the gravestone candle with a stop loss set on close above the highs of this candle, because that would invalidate the bearish signal.

If the third candle in the pattern fails to be a bearish candle that goes lower the next period, the gravestone candle could be invalidated. A winning short position could be allowed to run using either a close over the previous candle or a short-term moving average as a trailing stop. Look for profit targets in the context of the current chart pattern, like price dropping back to the 50 RSI, a previous support level or a key longer term moving average.

This IBM daily chart shows two examples of perfect gravestone doji candle patterns. The first is in the middle of the chart, followed by another at the end. We'll look at the first example. The bullish candle is followed by the gravestone doji reversal candle and a bearish candle lower. The three candles after the pattern formed didn't move above the high price of the gravestone doji, so a short position would have been safe until the gap down on the fourth day. This is another example of an an early warning bearish candle pattern before a big break to the downside.

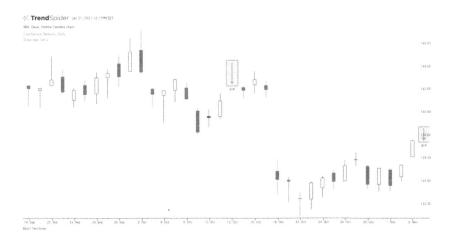

Chart courtesy of TrendSpider.com

23

BEARISH SPINNING TOP

BEARISH

spinning top

A bearish spinning top is a single candlestick pattern that's formed by a small body in the middle of long wicks. This pattern signals that buyers and sellers have no control of price action in the time frame of the candle.

- The spinning top candle indicates that price ended closer to the open or the close at the end of the period, rather than an extreme of the trading range.
- This shows the chart is indecisive on the current trend.
- The range of the candle's long wicks displays volatility. At different points in the time frame of the candle, both buyers and sellers had control, but failed to follow through and hold a swing or trend in price.
- A spinning top candle is primarily used in technical analysis as a signal that a trend is ending.
- If the spinning top candle forms after

a trend or swing in a market's price action, it can signal an increased probability of a reversal.

- It's an indecision candle with expanded volatility showing that the current direction of the move on the chart is losing momentum.

- When a spinning top occurs in an uptrend or upswing in price action, it may indicate that buyers are losing momentum and the chart could be near a short-term top. When a spinning top occurs during a downtrend or downswing in price action, it may indicate that sellers are losing momentum and the chart is near a short-term bottom. Of these two scenarios, the topping pattern is more common.

- Spinning top candles tend to be nearly symmetrical, with upper and lower wicks of approximately the same size.

- The body must be smaller than the wicks.

- The pattern shows indecision and greater odds of a reversal of the current trend or the possibility of sideways price action.
- This candle shows buyers losing conviction in an up move, or the charts running out of sellers at lower prices in a down move.
- Many traders wait for one more candle after the spinning top to confirm the reversal and increase the odds that the signal is valid.
- The body of the spinning top candle can be white or black with little difference in meaning.

Like all technical analysis, this pattern shows a higher probability that one thing will happen over another, but position sizing and stop losses are critical to manage the risk.

In this 65-minute Ford chart, the two consecutive bearish spinning top candles signaled no upside momentum and an ongoing trading range. After these spinning tops, the chart stayed in a range for eight days before finally breaking to the downside and falling out of the range. Remember that candles can signal loss of momentum as well as reversals and trends. Candlestick patterns can show the current path of least resistance, and sometimes that's just a sideways move.

Chart courtesy of TrendSpider.com

24

BEARISH KICKER

The bearish kicker is a two-candle pattern that starts with a large bullish candlestick higher, and then a second, large bearish candle that gaps lower in price and keeps going to the downside.

- The bearish candle can have a flat bottom and top or wicks, but from the bullish candle close to the bearish candle open, it should reflect a price gap.
- It isn't necessary for this pattern to form after a large downtrend or uptrend in price to indicate that a move to the downside may have started.
- If this pattern occurs as a reversal signal near the top of an uptrend, it can create a better risk/reward ratio when a short is entered there.
- It's a valid bearish signal whether the current chart is in an uptrend, downtrend or going sideways.

- This pattern is called a kicker because the price action resembles kicking something down a hill.
- This candle formation shows a bearish sentiment with no buyers inside the gap down in price action or as the candle continues to move lower.
- This candle is a gap down pattern in technical analysis, and it's one of the most bearish candlestick chart patterns showing momentum with sellers.
- This pattern shows both long positions being exited and possible short sellers coming in to push prices lower.
- This pattern is usually created be a negative news event that causes the next candle to quickly price the new information into the chart. It confirms the direction on a chart is now heading downward over the two-candle period.
- The bearish kicker can happen during

a price range on a chart signaling a break to the downside. When it happens during an upswing or uptrend in price action, it's a reversal signal. When it occurs during an existing downtrend in price, it's a continuation pattern.

- The bearish kicker is a momentum signal to the downside, regardless of the current chart pattern.

A bearish kicker candlestick pattern can signal that it's time to exit a long position at the end of the bearish candle that's the second candle in the pattern. It can also signal to short at the end of the bearish candle with a stop loss set above the high of the bearish candle.

In this 65-minute Goldman Sachs chart, the bearish kicker candle pattern signals a move to the downside. This was a great example of a clean move lower as price never rallied back to test the highs of the pattern. It immediately dropped lower, then went sideways before breaking to the downside. This is a rare bearish kicker pattern that rallies briefly through the price gap inside the period, but at the close it reflects a bearish kicker based on the opening and closing prices of the bearish candle.

Chart courtesy of TrendSpider.com

25

BEARISH ENGULFING

bearish BEARISH
engulfing

A bearish engulfing candle forms on a chart when a small bullish candle body is inside the larger range of the next large bearish candle.

- This pattern is considered a major bearish reversal signal on a chart, especially when it occurs near a peak in prices.
- When a two-candle bearish engulfing pattern happens near the top of a chart trending upward, or when a chart has an overbought technical reading like a 70 RSI or 3rd standard deviation from the 20-day moving average, there are greater odds of reversal.
- A bearish engulfing candle indicates that buyers rejected higher prices from the previous day and sellers stepped in to push prices down under the previous day's support.
- This is a double bearish candle because buyers couldn't hold the breakout to new highs over the

previous day's range, or hold the
previous day's low price.
- This pattern indicates the end of
buying pressure and the beginning of
selling pressure on the same candle.
- The bigger the bearish candle is
versus the previous candle, the more
meaningful it may be.
- The bearish engulfing candle has less
meaning in volatile and choppy
charts.
- There's a higher probability of a short
sell working with the bearish
engulfing signal if the trader waits for
the next candle to confirm the reversal
with a follow through bear candle.
- The context of where the engulfing
bearish candle appears is critical
because the meaning is more clear at
the end of an uptrend than when
inside an existing trading range.
- The more confluences of additional
bearish technical signals that occur
with this candle, the greater the odds
of it marking a top on a chart.

On this 65-minute 3M chart, the bearish body candle engulfs the smaller bullish candle body and price immediately drops after the pattern forms. A candle pattern can still be considered engulfing if the larger, bearish body fully engulfs the smaller bullish body, even with a higher wick on the smaller candle. On this chart, the price continues to fall until the big pin bar reversal candle forms eight periods later.

Chart courtesy of TrendSpider.com

26

BEARISH HARAMI

BEARISH

harami

A bearish harami candlestick pattern is created by two candles. The first candle is a large bullish candle, and the next is a small bearish candle.

- The full trading range of the opening and closing prices of the second smaller bearish candle must be completely engulfed inside the body of the first large bullish candle.
- The bearish inside candle of the pattern should be much smaller or about one-fourth the size of the bullish candle.
- This formation signals the probability that a reversal is about to occur during an uptrend.
- The size and range of the second bearish candle can be an indicator of the likelihood of a reversal. The smaller the bearish candle, the higher probability of a reversal happening because it shows buyers are absent at

higher prices and that price has lost momentum and stopped.

- The bearish harami can be a signal to lock in profits for long positions during uptrends because it indicates the uptrend may have ended with the rejection of higher prices for two consecutive days.
- The second bearish candle confirms that the high on the chart may be in. A short position trade can be taken at the end of the second bearish candle signal with a stop loss on a move or period close above that bearish candle.
- The probabilities of this signal being successful are increased if it occurs near an overbought or over extended area on a chart, or at three or more standard deviations from the 20-day moving average.
- This pattern has additional confirmation if the next candle after the first two is a bearish candle that opens lower.

- This pattern is best used as a bearish reversal candlestick pattern in an existing uptrend.
- A bearish harami cross is formed when the bearish candle in the pattern is a doji.
- The inverse of the bearish harami is the bullish harami.

In this 65-minute Pfizer chart example, the bearish harami formed near the top of the chart and price immediately dropped lower after this pattern. It stopped going down after setting lower lows for nine periods, and began going sideways as the downswing ended on the pin bar reversal candle.

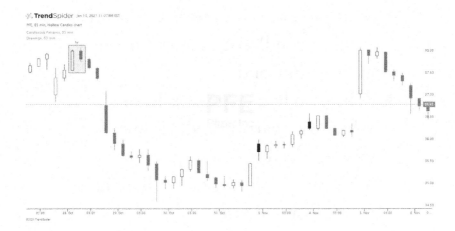

Chart courtesy of TrendSpider.com

DARK CLOUD COVER

BEARISH

dark cloud cover

The dark cloud cover is a bearish reversal candlestick pattern. It starts by appearing to continue an uptrend with a long white candle body, then price opens near or above the previous period highs on the next day. It then reverses and closes near the middle of the previous day's bullish candle range.

- At the peak of the pattern, there's a long bullish body candle that appears to be showing the continuation of a strong uptrend, but instead it's followed by a long body bearish reversal candle.
- This pattern indicates the shifting of a chart from bullish momentum to bearish. Buyers pushing prices higher gives way to selling pressure that stops the chart from holding new highs and drags prices lower.
- The second day reversal candle needs to be approximately halfway inside the previous day's trading range to validate this pattern.

- Many traders wait for an additional bearish candle lower to validate the up and then down candles as a reversal to prove its validity.
- The dark cloud cover candlestick pattern gets its name because it looks like an ominous overhead cloud.
- This pattern is bearish because it represents overhanging resistance on the chart and then rains down selling pressure.
- This is a bearish reversal pattern of a current uptrend.
- The two candles that create the pattern should have large bodies in relation to other nearby candles, indicating a large move in both directions, first up and then down.
- This pattern forming with smaller candles is less meaningful because there isn't much momentum to confirm the reversal.
- A third bearish candle that closes lower than the next day is the confirmation of a reversal in an

uptrend, and it's used as a short signal for many candlestick traders.

This Visa 65-minute chart shows two great examples of dark cloud cover candlestick patterns. There are immediate swings in price to the downside the period after they formed. Both times, the pattern was immediately followed by lower highs and lower lows that lead to a price drop for seven periods after the bearish candle signal. In both instances, the highs of the candle pattern were not broken to the upside to stop out a short position entered after the pattern formed. Allowing a winner to run with a trailing stop on a close above the previous day's high would have lead to good profits.

Chart courtesy of TrendSpider.com

28

TWEEZER TOP

BEARISH

tweezer top

The tweezer top candlestick pattern is created by two or more candles with matching highs in price. A tweezer top happens when two candlesticks form back-to-back or near each other with the same, or almost the same, highs.

- This pattern is more meaningful when it happens near overbought levels or key price resistance on a chart. It shows an absence of any buyers at higher prices of the two candles, for two periods after repeated attempts to move higher.
- The two candles that create this pattern don't have to be in consecutive order, and the size and colors can be different.
- The tweezer top candle signal is a high probability reversal signal that is more meaningful when it happens at a confluence of other signals on a chart like overbought, at the top of a

Bollinger Band, key price resistance or near a key overhead moving average.

- This pattern has additional confirmation when It's followed by a bearish candle pattern.

- This can be a sell signal for longs, or a sell short signal, because it indicates high probability of a reversal to the downside, as consecutive high prices hold as resistance and are rejected with a minimum of two candles.

- A tweezer top can be separated by a few candles, but the classic version of this pattern happens over two consecutive candles.

- While any color candles can create the pattern, it's more likely to see a reversal if the second candle of the tweezer top is bearish and down.

- This pattern signals that longs should take profit at the end of the second candle, and that shorts can step in and bet on lower prices at the end of the second candle, because buyers are absent at any higher prices.

A short sell trade entered after the second candle can set a profit target back to previous technical chart price support levels. A stop loss should be set to exit if price closes above the highs of the tweezer top candles.

This Microsoft 65-minute chart is an example of four tweezer top patterns. The first marks a high in price before it fell for three periods before rebounding. The second occurs in the middle of a trading range. The final two tweezer tops occur back-to-back, with the second making lower highs than the first before price dropped lower over the next four periods. Tweezer tops can show short-term resistance levels on a chart and are a warning sign, that at least in the short-term, selling pressure at the highs is moving price lower.

Chart courtesy of TrendSpider.com

29

BEARISH ABANDONED BABY

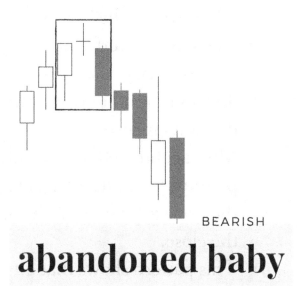

BEARISH

abandoned baby

The bearish abandoned baby is a three-candle pattern that typically follows an up-swing in price. It's created by a large, bullish up candle, followed by a gap up doji, and then a large bearish candle after a gap down in price.

- It gets its name from the look of the doji candle getting *abandoned* by the two larger surrounding candles, due to the gap up and then back down separating the doji body from the other two candle bodies.
- The most powerful form of this pattern is an *actual* gap between the doji and the other two candles, but that is a rare event.
- Most abandoned baby candlestick patterns have wicks that crossover in the price gap between the open and the close.
- This pattern shows that buyers have lost momentum as price stops rising as the doji is formed, volatility contracts

and sellers step in and bid down the price on the next candle.

- This pattern signals a high probability of the end of an uptrend in price and the potential for a move down in price action.
- This pattern can be followed by either a swing back down in price, or a new trading range forming after the reversal off the highs.
- Price should not rally back above the high of the last bearish candle in the pattern or it will invalidate the downside signal.

The common sell or sell short signal for this pattern is at the end of the third bearish candle. This can be a take profit signal on a long position or possibly a short sell signal. If this leads to a short sell signal, then a stop loss could be set above the high of the bearish candle that followed the doji.

A short trade should target a previous technical support level on a chart to lock in profits if a downswing or downtrend emerges after this pattern.

This Accenture daily chart shows examples of two bearish abandoned baby candlestick patterns. The first occurs followed by a swing down in price. The rally higher three days later didn't overtake the highs of the pattern before going lower. This kept the pattern valid for the move down. The second abandoned baby pattern formed at the top of an upswing in price with a bullish candle followed by the doji, and then a bearish candle lower before a move lower in price. Notice that this pattern can has candle wicks overlapping in the gap area. As mentioned previously, a pure abandoned baby with open gaps in price with no wicks in the gap area, is rare.

Chart courtesy of TrendSpider.com

30

THREE BLACK CROWS

BEARISH

three black crows

Three black crows is a bearish three candlestick chart pattern formed by price action closing lower than the open and below the previous day's low, for three days in row. It's created by three long bearish candlesticks that stair-step downward.

- Each candle in the pattern must open below the last day's high in price, at least in the middle of the previous price range of the previous day.
- The three candles should all close lower than the previous candle low so the last one sets a new short-term low price.
- This pattern can have small wicks but shouldn't have long lower or upper wicks.
- This pattern can signal a strong price action reversal from an uptrend to a downtrend on a chart.
- It can signal the end of an uptrend and the beginning of a new swing lower or a range-bound market. In the

short-term, it can signal the loss of upside momentum.

- The three black crows can signal a change in market sentiment from positive to negative.
- It's generally looked at on the daily chart for a longer term sentiment change due to the distribution.
- These candles start higher but end lower for the period, and many candlestick programs use solid red candles when price closes lower than the open.
- This pattern gets its name from the candles having an ominous look before flying down from their perch. The pattern will be red because they are bearish candles.
- It's important to take chart context into account. This bearish reversal pattern near a chart pattern top with an overbought technical reading will have more room to go lower than if this candle pattern forms at the end of

a long market sell-off into oversold conditions.
- The inverse of the bearish three black crows candle pattern is the bullish three white soldiers candle pattern.

This McDonald's 65-minute chart shows this pattern followed by one more strong down day, before reversing back into a range-bound market. This pattern occurred after two previous bearish candles had already formed and took the chart into a trading range. After six straight bearish candles, the odds were good that the price would bounce higher as it approached old resistance from the previous price range and it became the new support.

Chart courtesy of TrendSpider.com

31

EVENING DOJI STAR

BEARISH

evening doji star

The evening doji star pattern is a group of candlesticks that signal a high probability that a current uptrend in price could reverse. This is a bearish candlestick pattern created by three candles in a row that consist of a large bullish candlestick, a small doji candle that's usually bearish, followed by a bearish candlestick.

This is a potential technical indication that there's a likelihood of a future decline in price. It takes three periods of candles to fully form:

1. A large bullish candlestick.
2. A gap up and a small doji candlestick that can be bullish or bearish, and higher than the previous day.
3. A gap down and a large bearish candle that opens at a price lower than the previous day's candle, continues to fall and close lower than the open.

- This pattern has the most meaning after a strong uptrend and can signal the market is making a top.
- This candlestick chart pattern is used

by technical analysts to signal the timing for a short selling position entry, or as a warning that it's time to lock in long position profits.

- The evening doji star is not a common pattern, but it can be a meaningful signal showing a failure to find buyers at higher price levels.

- To increase the odds of succes, traders can use other indicators like overbought/oversold price oscillators, moving averages and trendlines to confirm a confluence for more meaning in the full chart context.

- An evening star pattern formed at an overbought RSI level, a key long-term moving average overhead or at an upper channel trendline has a higher probability of marking a chart top.

- If the second candle in this pattern is a doji, then it's called an evening doji star. The principles stay the same, if it doesn't have a doji as a middle candle, it's a normal evening star pattern.

- The inverse chart pattern of the

evening star is the morning star, that is viewed as a bullish reversal near a chart bottom.

This AT&T 65-minute chart has two patterns that qualify as evening star patterns. The first has an evening star pattern followed by a slow and choppy price swing lower, with the high prices of the pattern never being breached. The second evening star pattern was followed by a trading range before a sharp decline in price, 14 periods later. Both of these patterns did mark short-term highs in price action and were followed by price swings lower.

Chart courtesy of TrendSpider.com

Here is example of an evening doji star candle pattern on a Citigroup 65-minute chart. After the bearish pattern formed, a nine-period downswing in price action followed.

Chart courtesy of TrendSpider.com

III

NEUTRAL
CANDLESTICK
PATTERNS

32

NEUTRAL DOJI CANDLES

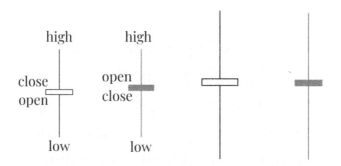

doji candlesticks

The doji is a neutral signal that occurs when a single candle has opening and closing prices that are close to the same, with a tiny body. In Japanese, *doji* means a mistake, implying that this candle is rare because it means both the buyers and sellers were mistaken about price.

A single doji means that buyers and sellers reached equilibrium during the candle period, ending at almost the same price from the beginning. This shows the opening buyers and sellers are in agreement with the closing buyers and sellers on chart price.

- When a doji appears inside an existing trading range, it reinforces that a chart is going sideways in price.
- When a doji appears near the end of an uptrend or downtrend, it may be signaling that the momentum of the trend is slowing or ending.
- Technical analysis considers the doji a reversal signal if it occurs at the end of a trend before the subsequent candle

confirms that a move is turning in the opposite direction.

- A doji shows that while price moved inside the trading period, it returned to where it started and invalidated both directional attempts.

- Doji stars have nearly the exact same open and close, giving them more of a line than a candle body. Doji stars are neutral patterns as individual candles, but can be part of more complex patterns. Surrounding candles give them meaning inside the context of a price move.

- Doji Stars are neutral when they occur inside trading ranges, they can be bearish as they occur at the end of an uptrend as price starts going lower. They can be bullish at the end of a downtrend if price then reverses and begins to go higher. During a trend, a doji star may mean a pause if the next candle continues to move in the direction of the current trend.

- This image demonstrates the doji star with the perfect *t* shape.

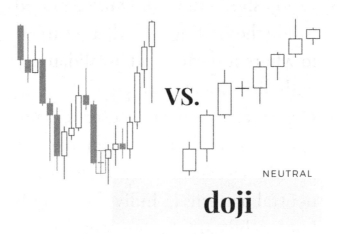

VS.

NEUTRAL

doji

Long-legged doji

The long-legged doji candlestick pattern has long upper and lower shadows (wicks) and generally has a closing price near where it opened in the time frame of the candle.

- Long-legged doji have long upper and lower wicks and tiny bodies, with the opening and closing price almost the same.
- This candle pattern signals indecision.

- It can be a reversal signal during strong trends.
- It can also signal a new range bound market.
- It can signal an expansion in volatility.
- Many traders wait for the next candle on the chart after the long-legged doji to confirm a reversal, because it creates a higher probability of success than signaling off just one candle.
- It is often caused by a news event that drives volatility expansion as the new information is priced into the chart.
- The odds of it being a reversal signal are higher when the long-legged doji candle occurs in an uptrend near an overbought reading, or if it appears in a downtrend near an oversold reading.

In this Johnson and Johnson 65-minute chart, the doji candles occur inside the existing trading range. They're neutral and give no price action signal.

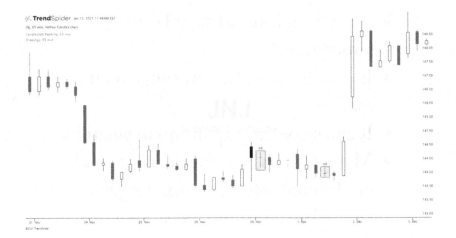

Chart courtesy of TrendSpider.com

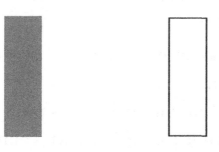

NEUTRAL

marubozu

The marubozu is a Japanese candlestick pattern used as a technical indicator of strong directional price action inside a specific period.

- The marubozu indicates that an asset has been bought or sold with momentum in one direction and closed near its high price or low price of the trading period.
- The marubozu candle is said to have a shaved top because the classic version has no wicks.
- It's also said to show dominance because the candle is larger and going in one direction.
- A marubozu consists primarily of a large candle body with almost no upper or lower wicks outside the top or bottom of the candle.
- The marubozu candlestick has a higher probability of success when it happens in confluence with other key

technical signals like moving averages, support, resistance or overbought/oversold readings.

- This candle is neutral and can be a reversal signal or a continuation candle depending on the context in the chart.
- The marubozu candle derives much of its signal value from the candles before and after it. It can confirm a trend or momentum or invalidate it.

A bullish marubozu candle has a long upward body and is created when the open is the low and the close is the high for the full trading period of the candle.

- The bullish marubozu shows that buyers were in control of the price of the asset from the opening trade to the closing trade.
- This is one of the most bullish individual candles in technical analysis, and it indicates a high

probability that the next candle on the chart will be bullish.

A bearish marubozu candle has a long downward body and is created when the open is the high and the close is the low for the full trading period of the candle.

- A bearish marubozu candlestick pattern shows that sellers were in control of the price of the asset from the opening trade to the closing trade.
- This is one of the most bearish individual candles in technical analysis and there's a high probability that the next candle on the chart will be bearish.

NEUTRAL

marubozu

This Hilton 65-minute chart had two marubozu candles form inside an upswing in price action that was setting higher highs before a sharp gap up and uptrend continuation. These two bullish marubozu gave an early strong bullish signal before the large move up occurred. The third marubozu on the chart occurred inside the range after the sell-off price peak, and was a bearish warning signal before a sharp move to the downside for the next eight periods. The fourth and last marubuzu occurred on the third from last period on the chart, before a small move higher in price. Marubuzu were strong momentum signals on this chart before the full moves occurred in both directions.

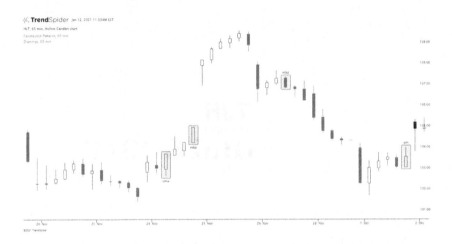

Chart courtesy of TrendSpider.com

CONCLUSION

A single candle for a trading period illustrates the open, the trading period and the close. When candles are combined, they create candlestick chart patterns that can indicate the current behavior of buyers and sellers on a chart over multiple trading periods.

These patterns don't predict the future as much as they show what is currently happening, but they can demonstrate the probabilities of what may happen next. Each entry signal using a candlestick chart pattern must also have exit signals. A profit target measures the potential for reward if the trade goes in your favor, while a stop loss sets your risk and keeps your losses small if the trade moves against you. Combined, they create your risk/reward ratio.

Candlesticks provide an edge of more than 50% that the next move in price action will go in the direction of the current move. However, the directional edge must be accompanied by managing the trade after entry so that it ends in one of four ways. The trade ends with a small loss, a small win, a breakeven or a large loss.

No trade using candlestick patterns should end in a large loss. The initial stop loss set at entry should be taken if it's triggered, eliminating the possibility of a large loss due to price action. The other part of risk management is proper position sizing. Your position size should be based on the maximum loss of trading capital you are willing to take if your stop loss is triggered.

Stop losses are best set at technical levels that invalidate the trade, like a close below the support of the candle that triggered the entry for a long position.

I use candlestick patterns inside the context of a chart's technical levels.

Here are other considerations to look for on a

chart to identify candlestick patterns inside the context of technical analysis. The odds of success increase for a candlestick pattern when they occur in confluence with a chart pattern.

Higher probability candlestick pattern parameters:

- Bullish reversals in downtrends that occur at the same level as a chart's price support.
- Bearish reversals in uptrends that occur at the same level as a chart's price resistance.
- Bullish continuations that occur breaking out of a chart's price resistance.
- Bearish continuations that occur breaking below a chart's price support.
- Neutral candles that occur inside a trading range confirm that the range will likely continue to go sideways.
- Neutral candles that occur inside a trend can be an early warning sign

that a trend may reverse or begin to go sideways.

- Bullish candlestick patterns that occur in overbought areas on a chart typically have a lower probability of creating a new, higher trend.

- Bearish candlestick patterns that occur in oversold areas on a chart typically have a lower probability of creating a new, lower trend.

- Bullish patterns have a higher probability of working out when price on a chart is also trending over the moving average for the time frame.

- Bearish patterns have a higher probability of working out when price on a chart is also trending under the moving average for the time frame.

- Over 90% of the time, price on a chart will stay within three standard deviations of the 20-day moving average. Most trends tend to lose their momentum once the third deviation is reached in either higher or lower extremes.

An edge in trading comes from structuring a trading strategy to make more money on winning trades than it costs for losing trades. Candlestick patterns can give you a quantified structure for entry signals, stop losses and trailing stops. These patterns can help you structure your trades in ways to create bigger wins than losses. Candlestick patterns can be a major part of a trader's system, along with other aspects of technical analysis.

Candlestick patterns can show the path of least resistance when taking trades that have the best probability for profitability. Candles can also indicate when the trade is not going to work out, and set a level to quickly exit when wrong.

There are no perfect trading strategies that let you win every time, there are only strategies that allow for bigger wins than losses. The best use of candlestick patterns is to use them to create great risk/reward ratios through your trade management of stop losses and trailing stops. Focus on bigger wins than losses and don't become overly concerned about winning percentage. The most important thing a trader can do is develop their own trading system that has an edge, and then trade it with discipline and proper position sizing to let their edge play out over time.

Candlestick charts patterns can be an important part of any trader's technical trading process. I know it has been an important part of my profitable trading strategy.

ACKNOWLEDGMENTS

TrendSpider.com used their excellent trading platform to create the historical chart images in this book. We're big fans of TrendSpider and recommend them to our students. Here are a few reasons we think their software is pretty great:

- Benzinga News Feed included (usually something that you have to buy)
- Analyst ratings
- Seasonality
- Anchored VWAP/Anchored Volume by Price

- Raindrops
- The Scanner and the Strategy Tester

A big thank you to the good folks at TrendSpider!

NEW TRADER U

Join thousands of trading students at New Trader University! Our eCourses are created for traders just starting out in the markets, and individuals looking to up their trading game.
Visit NewTraderUniversity.com to learn more about our eCourses today!

Don't forget that you can listen to many of our titles on Audible!

Read more of our bestselling titles:
The Ultimate Guide to Chart Patterns
The Ultimate Guide to Price Action Trading
The Ultimate Trading Risk Management Guide
The Ultimate Guide to Trading Psychology
The Working Dead
New Trader Rich Trader (Revised and Updated)
New Trader Rich Trader 2
So You Want to be a Trader
New Trader 101
Moving Averages 101: 2nd Edition
Options 101
5 Moving Averages That Beat Buy and Hold
Buy Signals and Sell Signals
Trading Habits
Investing Habits
Calm Trader

Made in the USA
Las Vegas, NV
05 October 2023

78609796R00108